MW01615454

WHAT O'...... ARE SAYING

My dear friend Dr Jason Hubbard has captured the heart of one of the great prayer and missions movements in church history. *Moravian Miracle* is fascinating reading, and deeply motivating. Let us follow in the footsteps of these courageous, prayer-devoted believers and finish the task of the great commission in our generation!

DR RICK WARREN
Author, The Purpose Driven Life
Executive Director, Finishing the Task Coalition
California, USA

The story of the Moravians' commitment to 24/7 prayer and its connection to missions in the 18th century has been an inspiration for my life personally, and for the ministry of IHOPKC. Thank you, Jason, for searching out this remarkable story that will surely add fuel to the fire of the rapidly accelerating 24/7 global prayer and missions movements in these days! I am grateful for you—that you lead so many into the reality that you live in, and that you share in such a compelling way in this new book. *Moravian Miracle* is a true gift to the global body of Christ.

MIKE BICKLE
Founder, International House of Prayer (IHOPKC)
Kansas City, USA

In an effort to help me make sense of a deep personal encounter with God, my mother gave me a book about Count Zinzendorf and the Moravians when I was 17 years old. It marked me for life. Now I am deeply grateful for Dr Jason Hubbard's new work, *Moravian*

Miracle. It recaptures the passion for Jesus and the joy in sacrifice that has gripped me for more than four decades. I pray it will do the same for you.

ERIC WATT

Founder and President, RUN Ministries
Virginia, USA

The Moravians have bequeathed rich legacies that outlive their generation. In *Moravian Miracle*, Dr Jason Hubbard rekindles the church's interest in the enduring legacies of the Moravians—namely, missions, 24/7 prayer and discipleship. God is using this book to awaken us and to popularize the enduring legacy of the Moravians in our generation. We must be conscious of that legacy and emulate it. This book is recommended for all who are involved in missions, intercession and the prayer movements.

AUSTEN UKACHI

Co-Ordinator, Strategic Prayer Network of MANI
Lagos, Nigeria

Every follower of Christ needs to read this book! Jason Hubbard is a Moravian scholar who captures for us the history of a 100-year prayer movement that changed the world. It is a roadmap for the revival we are crying out for today.

CHERYL SACKS

Co-Founder, BridgeBuilders International
Arizona, USA

Who are the Moravians and how did this humble band of Christ-followers have such a remarkable impact on the history of Protestant missions? In this accessible introduction, Dr Jason Hubbard provides a spiritually rich reading of the foundational years of the Moravian community and the prayer revival that sparked the world mission movement almost three centuries ago. The past several decades have seen a flourishing of 24/7 prayer movements, and we would be wise to follow Dr Jason Hubbard in looking to the Moravians for clues concerning how 'prayer canopies' can be multiplied across the globe today. Each chapter in this study concludes with insightful discussion questions, making *Moravian Miracle* an ideal resource for new and veteran prayer groups. This resource is sure to stir, inspire, and get us asking how, through prayer, God might be leading the church across the entire world into the greatest revival in history.

DR JONATHAN ARMSTRONG
Professor of Bible and Theology, Moody Bible College
Illinois, USA

I know of no leader better equipped to write a book on the Moravians than my dear friend, Dr Jason Hubbard. Jason has lived a Moravian lifestyle of radical devotion to Jesus, prayer, and mission. This book will inspire you, convict you, challenge you, and motivate you.

BRIAN ALARID
President, America Prays and World Prays
Chairman, Pray For All
Texas, USA

Moravian Miracle by Dr Jason Hubbard is a must-read for every Christian longing to grow spiritually, dive into the presence of God, encounter His Spirit, and live a life devoted to prayer. Hubbard gives you five practical tips to apply in your daily life on how to learn from the outstanding success of the Moravians, who did indeed change the world. This book will be a game-changer in bringing revival to your Christian life.

WERNER NACHTIGAL
International President, GO Movement
Berlin, Germany

For many years our ministry has been deeply moved by the extraordinary story of Count Zinzendorf and the Moravian revival, with team members spending time in prayer at Herrnhut. This book gives an excellent account of all that took place as the Moravians humbly walked the way of the Cross. It is full of Kingdom keys from the past that will continue to unlock doors in the future for the glory of the Lamb of God.

PS JENNY HAGGER AM
Founder, Australian House of Prayer for All Nations
Founder, Mission World Aid
Adelaide, Australia

Looking for personal revival? Start here. I was 18 years old when I first read about the Moravian prayer movement and it changed my vision for prayer forever. Ultimately, it was the Moravians who inspired me to launch PULSE, and this inspiration has remained in every effort we have undertaken since. Read *Moravian Miracle*, and be inspired and reminded that the prayer closet is the backbone of every movement of God. A prayer meeting that started 300 years ago is still changing the world today!

NICK HALL
Founder and President, PULSE
Minnesota, USA

Moravian Miracle is a brilliant addition to the growing body of work documenting the amazing, prayer-fueled Moravian missions movement. I first read about the Moravians in 1995, and my first reaction as an avid student of revival history was to ask, "Why has no one ever told me about the Moravians before?" Since then, I have read everything I could get my hands on about the Moravians. In this devotional book, Dr Jason Hubbard has broken new ground and given us the secrets behind the 'Moravian miracle'. Any Christian with a passion for prayer and missions must read this book. Taking this one step further, any believer who wants to put Jesus' words into action must read this book!

WARWICK MARSH
Faith and Family Advocate, Canberra Declaration
Wollongong, Australia

The Moravian story is a miracle! *United*—as a community with God and each other. *Strategic*—taking His love to the ends of the earth. *Sustainable*—an inter-generational prayer meeting and mission movement that lasted for over 100 years and changed the world. Thank you, Jason, for sharing this amazing story with such insight and clarity. I want to share it with all of my friends, everywhere!

TOM VICTOR
President, The Great Commission Coalition
Texas, USA

Thank you so much, brother Jason, for giving us the amazing gift of *Moravian Miracle*. I have always been intrigued by the statement, "May the Lamb who was slain receive the reward for His suffering," which I first heard from you when we met in 2017 in Herrnhut. After reading this book, I know that you have been smitten by the Lamb's extravagant love in His suffering and sacrifice. Another favourite phrase of yours is "Behold the Lamb!" As you have been in this intimate posture of beholding the Lamb all these years, the Lord Jesus has graced you to write such a masterpiece. The last prayer you wrote in this book will challenge each one of us to seriously abandon ourselves to the Lamb of Love, who is the center of all of our worship, all of our obedience, and all of our affections. He alone is worthy.

REV ANN LOW
Executive Member, International Prayer Connect
Co-Founder, Hand in Hand with Families in Prayer
Kuala Lumpur, Malaysia

If you sense a spiritual yearning in your soul calling you to a deeper and more fruitful life in Christ, this book is for you. Although you may not know how this deeper life could look, or how to live the crucified life, *Moravian Miracle* provides a heart-moving picture that will ignite your soul. As I read this book, I found myself going back over passages, once, then twice, then again more slowly as it resonated deeply and fanned a flame in my heart. I took notes, reflected on quotes and accounts, and prayed the beautiful prayers contained in these pages. The testimony of the Moravians' humility, gentleness and servitude challenged me greatly. I will be recommending this book to all of our young missionaries.

CINDY McGARVIE
National Director, Youth for Christ
Brisbane, Australia

Jason is a man of prayer who connects and facilitates people across the globe in prayer and fellowship, and who releases others in their gifts. It was an absolute joy to read *Moravian Miracle*. The book is informative, inspirational, and challenges us to a deeper prayer life. What stood out to me more than anything was the link between prayer and our Christian witness; and the long-term, global impact of the Moravians that is still being felt today. This book is a must-read for anyone interested in increasing their prayer life and having a deeper walk with God.

KYM FARNIK
Executive Member, Australia Prays
Adelaide, Australia

Part history, part devotional, part prayer guide, all fire, *Moravian Miracle* is a profound little book that will change the way you think about prayer and missions. Dr Jason Hubbard doesn't just tell the story of the Moravians in these pages. He burns with the passion that ignited them—an all-consuming zeal for the glory of the Lamb. The Moravians really did change the world. The message of Jason's book is that, by God's grace, we can do it again.

KURT MAHLBURG
Author, Cross and Culture
Research and Features Editor, Canberra Declaration
Sydney, Australia

Joining believers around the world in celebrating the 300-year anniversary of the founding of the remarkable community of Herrnhut this year, I can only marvel at how God moved this small community into a season of united prayer that would change history and influence some of greatest leaders and movements in

Christian history. The question Dr Jason Hubbard asks in this powerful book rings true for all of us today: *What would it look like to see a modern-day Moravian movement initiated and sustained in our day?* This well-researched account of the history and influence of the Moravians and their leader, Count Nikolaus von Zinzendorf, is a gem that will encourage those hungry for more of the presence of God in their lives to seek a fresh encounter with His Spirit. Moreover, it will carry forward their legacy of prayer, missions and discipleship in our day. May that which Zinzendorf and his companions modelled truly become a catalyst for revitalizing and unifying the global church. And may we heed the call to return to our first love, as the bell of awakening is heard ringing across the nations in this hour.

ANJA LETSATSI
Global Voice of Prayer
Cape Town, South Africa

You are interested in reading this book? Wait a minute. This book isn't simply about history. It is about *His* story, and possibly your story. It doesn't simply contain facts, it contains factors—factors that could change your life. It is not simply words on a page—it could be a word for you. And it is really more about the future than it is about the past. You see, the *Moravian Miracle* happened many years ago, but it is stirring again, and the Lord may use this little book to make a big change in you—and through you, to make a big change in the world. Don't approach this book like other books. Don't just anticipate knowing more. Anticipate doing more because of what you will know. What happened in and through the Moravians was very unusual, but it shouldn't be. It happened a long time ago but it can also happen again—this time, not through them, but through you. And with God's help, and your willingness to let Him speak to you through what Dr Jason Hubbard has written, this book may not be the last chapter of the *Moravian Miracle*.

DENNIS FUQUA
Director, International Renewal Ministries
Washington, USA

Moravian Miracle

The 100 Year Prayer Meeting
That Changed the World

DR JASON HUBBARD

First published in Australia in 2022

Australian Heart Publishing
PO Box 378
Unanderra NSW 2526
Phone/Fax: (02) 4272 9100

Printed May 2022

ISBN: 978-1-922480-25-5
eBook ISBN: 978-1-922480-26-2

Cover design by Kurt Mahlburg

Edited by Kurt Mahlburg

Printed in Australia by
Peacemakers Ministries
60 King Street
Warrawong NSW 2502

*For my precious wife Kristie Hubbard, to whom
I am deeply indebted. You have been my greatest
supporter, personal intercessor and best friend.*

CONTENTS

Foreword   1

Introduction   5

CHAPTER ONE
The Hidden Seed   9

CHAPTER TWO
The Passion of Zinzendorf   17

CHAPTER THREE
Summer of Revival   27

CHAPTER FOUR
Fire on the Altar   35

CHAPTER FIVE
Lord of the Harvest   39

CHAPTER SIX
Awakening a Giant   45

CHAPTER SEVEN
Let the Nations Be Glad   53

CHAPTER EIGHT
Five Marks of the Moravians   65

About the Author   81

Notes   91

Foreword

As a leader who has been involved in missions for over half a century, and as someone who has repeatedly witnessed the power of prayer as it impacts missionary advances globally, I contend that there is no story greater than that of the 18th-century Moravian missions movement. At the heart of that movement was earnest, persistent, 24/7 prayer: over 100 years of non-stop seeking God for the fulfilment of His purposes on earth.

The book you hold in your hands, *Moravian Miracle*, powerfully retells the Moravians' story and plants a seed of hope and anticipation that a new movement of similar global, continuous prayer will soon usher in the greatest harvest of souls in the history of the church.

If you have heard this story before, you need to hear it again. There are essential details you may have missed. If the story is new to you, you need to hear it for the first time. That's because, as I firmly believe, *God wants to do it again.* You can't afford to miss being a part of it. Every spiritual indicator suggests there is a re-birthing of a new Moravian-like movement of continuous, global, harvest-focused prayer growing in the womb of God's presence worldwide. It is certain to transform nations. Seriously, there's another 'Moravian miracle' on its way.

God has led one of today's most respected global prayer leaders, Dr Jason Hubbard, to retell the Moravian story. As I read Hubbard's freshly penned account, I learned even more about how this movement began and how it grew out of a band of persecuted believers—spiritual misfits, you might say—in the early 1700s.

The movement started with a wealthy nobleman, Nikolaus Ludwig von Zinzendorf, who grew up in a religious family that became Lutheran during the Reformation. Spiritually sensitive, even as a child of just six, young Nikolaus would often write love letters to Jesus, climb the castle tower, and toss them out the window. It was to be a precursor to how Zinzendorf would be used of the Lord to ignite one of the great missionary enterprises of history. And it would happen during one of the most challenging eras for missionaries to be sent to the ends of the earth.

Zinzendorf owned a large estate in Saxony, modern-day Germany. He named it Herrnhut, meaning, "watch of the Lord." Founded in 1722, Herrnhut soon became home to several hundred persecuted Christians from Bohemia and Moravia. The community hardly lived up to its name for the first five years. Dissension and hostility permeated the atmosphere. Finally, in early 1727, Zinzendorf and several others—including the leader of the persecuted believers, an itinerant carpenter—agreed together to seek God earnestly for revival. That revival came dramatically in August of 1727. The fruit of that revival grew globally, fueled and sustained by continuous, non-stop prayer for more than a century.

I'll let Jason Hubbard tell you the rest of the story. But I can assure you of this: although many church historians would later refer to William Carey as the father of modern missions, it is noteworthy that 60 years before Carey sailed for India in 1793, the Moravians had already sent out over 300 missionaries to the ends of the earth. Over the following 150 years, they would commission 2,158 foreign missionaries: an unprecedented number for that era in history. This is their story. On the 300th anniversary of the birth of the Moravian missions movement, Jason Hubbard believes God wants to do it again. Best of all, God invites you to be a part of the story!

DICK EASTMAN
International President, Every Home for Christ
President, America's National Prayer Committee

Introduction

The story of Count Zinzendorf and the Moravians is one of the most inspiring in all of church history. These humble believers were used by God to establish the first Protestant prayer movement that operated 24 hours a day, seven days a week. The Lord also used them to pioneer the first Protestant missionary movement, which saw them take the gospel to the ends of the earth. Their heart was to see a believer, a body of Christ, and a Bible in the heart language of the people—for everyone, everywhere in the world.

I believe that the 18th century Moravians and their leader, Count Nikolaus von Zinzendorf, are outstanding models for us to learn from. May their example spur us on in our growth together as Christ-exalting, Spirit-led, Bible-based, gospel-dominated, disciple-making, love-saturated believers who follow the Lamb wherever He goes!

This year marks the 300-year anniversary of the founding of Herrnhut, the location where the Moravian miracle unfolded. On June 17th, 1722, Christian David felled the first tree for the first home in Herrnhut. He dedicated this small community to the Lord, praying from Psalm 84:3-4:

> Even the sparrow finds a home, and the swallow a nest for herself, where she may lay her young, at your altars, O LORD of hosts, my King and my God. Blessed are those who dwell in your house, ever singing your praise!

Indeed, this small community would eventually become a dwelling place for the Lord, and an altar for the presence of the Lord.

A Timeline of the Moravians

1700. Nikolaus von Zinzendorf is born into a wealthy Lutheran Pietist family.

1722. Zinzendorf allows persecuted Christians, coming from parts of modern-day Czech Republic, Poland and Germany, to settle on his property in Herrnhut.

1727. Many prayer gatherings and personal conversations take place. On August 13th, when the inhabitants take communion together, the Holy Spirit brings reconciliation, unity, and a common focus on the Lamb and their love for one another.

1727. Just 14 days after their special communion service, the Moravians begin to take turns to pray and worship, day and night. This 24/7 prayer chain continues for at least 100 years.

1732 onwards. Herrnhut sends missionaries to the Caribbean, Greenland, America, India, Africa, and many other lands. The Moravians are willing to give their whole lives for the cause of the gospel. During this time, the Moravian watchword is formulated: "May the Lamb who was slain receive the reward for His suffering."

1760. Nikolaus von Zinzendorf dies.

Our Lamb Has Conquered

In this short volume, it is our hope to capture the heart of the Moravians. We will discuss the early days of the movement, the passion of Zinzendorf, the 'summer of revival' in 1727, the 100-year prayer meeting, the impact of the Moravian missions movement throughout the world, and five lessons that we can learn from the Moravians and apply today. I want to encourage you to ask this question as you are reading:

What would it look like to see a contemporary Moravian movement initiated and sustained in our day?

So many people throughout church history have been inspired by the Moravians' 100 years of prayer; their dedication to missions; and their whole-hearted love for Jesus Christ.

On August 13th, 1727, the Moravians experienced a powerful visitation of the Holy Spirit during a communion service. It was described as a 'baptism of love', where God's love was shed abroad in their hearts and poured out in love for one another (cf. Romans 5:5). Following this, the Holy Spirit compelled them to build a canopy of united, strategic and sustainable prayer that continued for a hundred years. As they prayed day and night—an initiative that included men, women, and children—God began to mark missionaries and send them to the nations of the earth. In all, 226 missionaries responded before Zinzendorf's death in 1760, ultimately helping to establish over 5,000 missionary settlements around the world.

What compelled them to pray around the throne, around the clock and around the globe, and then to be sent on gospel mission, was the absolute worth of Jesus. Their purpose and mandate was to win for the Lamb who was slain the due reward for His suffering. They often would cry out, "Our Lamb has conquered, let us follow Him." This vision came from Revelation 5:12, which declares:

> Worthy is the Lamb who was slain, to receive power and wealth and wisdom and might and honor and glory and blessing!

Prayer

As we begin to read this story, Father of glory, may You pour out the Spirit of wisdom and of revelation in the knowledge of Your Son. Would You enlighten the eyes of our understanding that we might know the hope to which You have called us, what are the riches of Your glorious inheritance in us, and what is the immeasurable greatness of Your power toward us who believe! In Jesus' name we pray, Amen. (Ephesians 1:17-19).

CHAPTER ONE

The Hidden Seed

Dating from 1722, the Moravian story is the fruit of three converging factors. The first was a religious revival in Germany called Pietism, which brought about the Christ-centered awakening of a dogma-driven church that was desperately in need of renewal. The second factor was the pressure of religious persecution and increasing division amongst God's people on the continent of Europe. The third was the personality and call of a man by the name of Nikolaus von Zinzendorf.

The Reformation—the 16th-century awakening that sought to correct church errors and abuses, led by Zwingli, Luther, Calvin, Bucer and others—was like an unquenchable fire bringing God's people back to the heart of the gospel and the authority of the written Word. The churches that arose out of the Reformation had done much to improve the religious life of

Europe. In the aftermath, however, much dissension arose, especially surrounding the organizational structure of the church, and endless theological debates.

Not only did major tensions continue between Catholics and Protestants, but also among the four major Protestant divisions: Lutherans, Reformed, Anabaptists, and Anglicans. Despite Luther's conviction, and his attempt to promote the doctrine of the priesthood of all believers, the Lutherans of the day were still heavily influenced by the state and by church leadership. The majority of believers in the body of Christ were still passive listeners and not active participants in God's kingdom. The church was yet to see every member on mission. The sacraments had become liturgical formalities without power. Moreover, the Thirty Years' War brought massive devastation to the cause of Christ.

Yet in the midst of these circumstances, a revival burst forth which came in the form of Pietism. This took place under the pastoral leadership of Philipp Jakob Spener, who introduced small home meetings in 1670, and wrote his seminal work *Pia Desideria* in 1675. Pietism helped believers recover a personal, experiential relationship with Jesus Christ, and the inward life of the Spirit that Luther had originally known.

Two centers of theological training emerged in Germany. The first was in Wittenberg, the center of orthodoxy. The second was in Halle, which became the center for Pietism. Zinzendorf was a child of Pietism, and yet he was a bridge between solid Lutheran doctrine, orthodox truth, and Pietism. Zinzendorf was a true forerunner, calling the church back to a personal and intimate relationship with Jesus Christ in the power of the Spirit.

For Zinzendorf, the essence of the Christian life was a gospel-centered, loving relationship with Jesus Christ. From an early age, he decided that his life-motto would be, "I have one passion: it is Jesus, Jesus only."

The Spiritual Father of the Moravians

I believe the origins of the Moravian movement can be traced back even earlier, through the leadership and ministry of John Hus. A spiritual father of the Moravian movement, Hus is considered by many historians to be the first true reformer of the church, preceding Martin Luther by a century. He was born in 1369 in the township of Husinec, in the Kingdom of Bohemia, in what is today the Czech Republic. Hus is sometimes referred to as a "Goose in Gooseland," owing to his surname, which means *goose*, and the township of his birth. Writes Rick Joyner:

> John Hus was a priest, pastor, professor, and philosopher, but his greatest impact was as a teacher and author devoted to biblical truth [...] Hus' preaching and teaching impact in the days before the invention of the printing press was unrivalled, with the possible exception of John Wycliffe. Virtually all the Reformers following Hus acknowledged him as their inspiration.[1]

In essence, the message of John Hus was the importance of getting the Word of God back into the hands of the common people. He also taught the doctrine of the priesthood of all believers, and the essential doctrines of the Christian faith that were summed up so well later in the *five solas*. The *five solas* were five Latin phrases or slogans that emerged during the Reformation to summarize the Reformers' theological convictions about the essentials of Christianity—namely, that we are saved by *grace alone* through *faith alone* in *Christ alone*, based on the authority of the *Scriptures alone*, and all for the *glory of God alone*.[2]

Hus became the University of Prague's rector in 1402. At the time, the University of Prague was one of the world's premier institutions of higher learning. During the same year, Hus was also appointed as the preacher at the newly constructed Bethlehem Chapel. It was from this pulpit that Hus began calling for the reformation of the church. He had a revolutionary, scriptural vision of what the church should look like, and this is what he preached. The Roman Catholic Church had banned the writings of the English reformer John Wycliffe. But this didn't deter Hus, who taught from Wycliffe's writings and translated them into Czech. Hus defended Wycliffe's works with such tenacity that one historian called Hus "Wycliffe's bulldog."[3] Hus staunchly argued against indulgences; advocated for both the bread and the wine to be served in communion (the Roman church was no longer offering the cup to the people); and preached in the common language of the people, as opposed to the untranslated Latin of the day.

John Hus also preached against the moral debauchery of the priests, bishops, cardinals, and even the Pope. He strongly stood against the selling of indulgences—the selling of the grace of God, including deliverance from purgatory, for money—as a perversion of biblical faith and an insult to God.

Hus' message became extremely popular. It soon spread into the surrounding lands of modern-day Poland, Hungary, Croatia, and Austria. Before long, Hus was called to appear before the Council of Constance by church leaders who felt threatened by those demanding reformation. Hus did not want to see the church torn apart: his heart was for reformation in the body of Christ. So he agreed to attend the Council, a decision buoyed by the guarantee of his safe passage there and back from his king. Nevertheless, for the sin of challenging the Roman church, Hus was declared a heretic at the Council of Constance in 1415, and was burned at the stake. Rick Joyner explains:

> Before the flames could take his life, Hus prophesied that the message of liberty and spiritual reform would not die. Instead, it would be "a hidden seed," falling into the ground and dying for a season, but one day sprouting and bearing much fruit.
>
> Church officials were convinced that Hus' message would die with him. To their dismay, his heroic death only fanned the flame his message had ignited. Truth is more powerful than death, and persecution only scatters the seeds of truth over a greater dis-

tance. Hus' courage and resolve to die rather than compromise his convictions inspired countless other martyrs after him.[4]

The hidden seed of John Hus—the power and clarity of his message, and his uncompromising devotion to the Scriptures—was carried in the hearts of many great saints who guarded it until the opportune time. One who followed in Hus' spiritual lineage was John Amos Comenius, who ultimately became a key inspiration for Zinzendorf.

Just prior to being burned at the stake, Hus was asked to recant his teachings. He responded:

> My Lord Jesus Christ was bound with a harder chain than this for my sake, and why then should I be ashamed of this rusty one? [...] I never preached any doctrine of an evil tendency; and what I taught with my lips I now seal with my blood.[5]

Hus then said to his executioner, "You are now going to burn a goose, [referring to the meaning of *Hus* in the Bohemian language] but in a century you will have a swan whom you can neither roast nor boil."[6]

As the flames climbed higher, Hus sang and it was reported that people could hear his song through the crackling of the fire.

After Hus' death, outrage filled Bohemia. In his name, followers revolted against Rome in violent protest that lasted for over a decade.

The Goose and the Swan

Almost exactly 100 years later, on October 31st in 1517, the great Reformer Martin Luther posted his 95 Theses on the door of the Castle Church in Wittenberg. After his death, Luther was frequently represented by a swan in Lutheran art. This is why Lutheran Press still today bears the swan logo and proudly continues to "Trumpet the Swan!"

In 1628, Johann Amos Comenius (1592–1670), the last Bishop of the United Brethren in Moravia, who is also considered to be the father of modern Christian education, led a small band of exiled believers over the border into Poland. They were escaping persecution in their homeland, and their community of faith seemed to be slowly dying out. As Comenius stood at the border, he raised his eyes to heaven and uttered a historic prayer. He prayed that God would "preserve a remnant, a hidden seed, which would one day spring up and grow into a great tree for the glory of God."[7]

A hidden seed did indeed spring up. Fifty years after Comenius' death, a remnant from the United Brethren crossed the border into Germany in 1722 and established the Moravian community of Herrnhut. Under the leadership of Count Zinzendorf, what that community became—and what it carried—continues to affect prayer, missions and discipleship movements around the world today.

Prayer

Lord, we thank You for the hidden seed of prayer, missions, and discipleship that You have preserved throughout the ages. We ask You to show us what our role is in carrying on the legacy of the Moravians.

Reflection and Bible Study

Matthew 16:25 *"For whoever would save his life will lose it, but whoever loses his life for my sake will find it."*

Q. What inspires you most about John Hus and the courage of his conviction?

Romans 12:1-2 *"I appeal to you therefore, brothers, by the mercies of God, to present your bodies as a living sacrifice, holy and acceptable to God, which is your spiritual worship. Do not be conformed to this world, but be transformed by the renewal of your mind, that by testing you may discern what is the will of God, what is good and acceptable and perfect."*

Q. In what areas in your life do you want to see growth to carry on the legacies of John Hus, John Comenius, and Zinzendorf?

CHAPTER TWO

The Passion of Zinzendorf

C ount Zinzendorf was a wealthy aristocrat, a nobleman by birth. In contrast to the rich young ruler who said "no" to Jesus in Mark 10:17-27, some call Zinzendorf 'the rich young ruler who said *yes*,' since he willingly gave up his wealth for the sake of the gospel, and to follow the Lamb wherever He goes.

Zinzendorf was born in Dresden and had a godly praying grandmother. He came to Christ at a young age, and even in his youth was often found in prayer meetings, following in his grandmother's footsteps. He wrote of his early experience of friendship with Jesus:

> I have had the happiness of knowing the Savior by experience from my youngest years [...] I have carried on a friendship with Him, quite in a childlike way, sometimes talking with Him for

whole hours as we talk with a friend, going in and out of the room quite lost in my meditations.[8]

When Zinzendorf was a teenager, he had a powerful encounter with the Lord. In a gallery in Dusseldorf, he saw a painting of the crucified Christ and stared at it for many hours. He saw the blood dripping from every wound; the love glowing in every tear; the grace shining in every brushstroke. The artist behind the painting had been saved by Jesus from a life of deep darkness and sin, and now he painted mercy in every line and forgiveness in every blood drop. At the bottom of the painting were etched the words,

All this I did for thee, What hast thou done for Me?[9]

On reading these words, Zinzendorf fell to his knees, sobbing. With all his heart, he promised that for the rest of his life, he would glorify the Lamb for what He had suffered on the cross. Zinzendorf had been wounded by the Wounded One, pierced through by the Pierced One, and scarred by the revelation of the sacrifice of the Son of God!

A life of disciplined prayer flowed naturally out of Zinzendorf's passionate love for Jesus Christ. We know that:

Count Zinzendorf had early on learned the secret of prevailing prayer. So active had he been in establishing circles for prayer that on leaving the college at 16 years of age, he handed his professor a list of seven praying societies.[10]

Order of the Mustard Seed

In 1716, Zinzendorf helped to form a group of school friends at the Halle Academy, in the east of Germany. They described themselves as the "Order of the Mustard Seed" and saw their society as a kind of spiritual order of knighthood. They dedicated their lives not to personal honor or self-advancement but to the radical service of Jesus Christ.[11] The rules they committed to live by would change and mature as the Order grew, but the heart of their promise always remained the same:

> *To Be True to Christ*
> *To Be Kind to People*
> *To Take the Gospel to the Nations*

For these young men, *true to Christ* meant growing in personal holiness, and walking with integrity and the truth of God's written Word in the midst of suffering and opposition. *Kind to people* included a commitment to helping the poor and broken, including praying for and serving their enemies. And their desire to take the *gospel to the nations* would lead to pioneering missionary work, making disciples across Europe, and eventually expanding their missionary efforts to every part of the known world.

After he left school, Zinzendorf took a year to travel around Europe, visiting various religious leaders, including Cardinal de Noailles, with whom he was "united in his love for the cross and the wounds of Christ." De Noailles also joined the Order of the Mustard Seed.

Although Zinzendorf was the godson of Philipp Jakob Spener, and raised in a strong Pietist tradition, he had been born into Austrian nobility—and therefore as a Count, he was expected to follow his late father's footsteps into government. Zinzendorf did as he was told, and in October 1721, he became the king's judicial counsellor at Dresden.

After less than a year at court, Zinzendorf bought the estate of Berthelsdorf from his grandmother, hoping to form a Christian community for oppressed religious minorities.

Herrnhut: The Watch of the Lord

Zinzendorf's estate at Berthelsdorf was located in what is now the south-east corner of Germany, near the border with Poland and the Czech Republic. Together with a friend and two local pastors, he formed another society, 'The League of Gentlemen.' The purpose of this new society was to "proclaim the mystery and charm of the incarnation," to establish schools and a printing press, and to form a small group network in the area.[12]

In 1722, Zinzendorf married his first wife, Erdmuth Dorothea, who was the Countess of Reuss-Ebersdorf. They lived together in Berthelsdorf in their manor house. A few years later, they built another manor house in Herrnhut, which was completed in 1727. Of their twelve children, only four reached adulthood.

Only three—Benigna, Agnes, and Elizabeth—were to outlive their parents.[13]

This same year, 1722, a group of Bohemian Moravians fleeing persecution came to meet with Zinzendorf, many of them risking their lives on the journey. They were descendants of the Waldensians. What set the Waldensians apart was their simple lives, their insistence on having the Bible in their mother tongue as their highest authority, their refusal to swear allegiance to King or State (which they expressed as "no other king but Jesus"), and their practice of taking both bread and wine for the Lord's Supper.

This group was led by Christian David, a carpenter. Christian David was called the 'Moravian Moses,' a name he earned by escorting families back and forth from Moravia to Zinzendorf's estate some ten times. When the first families arrived with Christian David, the area didn't show much promise. There were no homes and very little water. But there was freedom, unlike their previous home—and they embraced it. As J.E. Hutton writes of this group of Waldensians:

> Some were imprisoned, some were loaded with chains; some were yoked to the plough, and made to work like horses; and some had to stand in wells of water till nearly frozen to death.[14]

One of their leaders, George Jaeschke, shared with his sons and grandsons before his passing:

> It is true that our liberties are gone, and that our descendants are giving way to a worldly spirit, so that the Papacy is devouring

them. It may seem as though the final end of the Brethren's Church has come. But, my beloved children, you will see a great deliverance. The remnant will be saved. How, I cannot say; but something tells me that an exodus will take place; and that a refuge will be offered in a country and on a spot where you will be able, without fear, to serve the Lord according to His holy Word.[15]

The time of their deliverance had come. Christian David heard of these sufferings and offered to come to their aid and rescue. David was introduced to Zinzendorf and asked the Count for permission to bring some persecuted refugees from Moravia to find refuge on his estate. The heart of the Count was moved, and he agreed. J.E. Hutton wrote of the occasion:

> The joyful carpenter returned to Moravia, and told the news to the Neisser family at Sehlen. "This," said they, "is God's doing; this is a call from the Lord."[16]

On June 8th, 1722, a small band of emigrants arrived at Zinzendorf's estate in Berthelsdorf after a long and wearying journey, with Christian David at their head. The rest of the group consisted of Augustin and Jacob Neisser along with their wives and children; Martha Neisser; and Michael Jaeschke, a cousin of the family. They left their homes in hopes of discovering God's will.

When these Moravian refugees first arrived in Berthelsdorf where Zinzendorf lived, they discovered that Zinzendorf was out of town. So instead, they met with the manager of Zinzendorf's estate, a man by the name of Heitz. Heitz was a godly man like Zinzendorf, and he blessed them to stay on Zinzendorf's land.

Heitz led these weary travelers to a dismal, swampy stretch of ground about a mile from Berthelsdorf. It was part of Zinzendorf's estate, and it lay at the top of a gentle slope, up which a long road now leads. It was a piece of common pasture ground, and was therefore known as the Hutberg, meaning the *Watch Hill*. Previously it had been used by gypsies and peddlers as a camping ground, and was in poor condition.

Concerned for their well-being, Heitz inspected the land with Christian David, and found a spot where a thick mist was rising, concluding that in this place a spring was sure to be found where a well could be dug. He offered a prayer on their behalf: "Upon this spot, in Thy name, I will build for them the first house."

Heitz inspected the site with Christian David, and marked the trees he might fell. Encouraged, Christian David grabbed his axe, struck it into a tree, and as he did so exclaimed from Psalm 84:3, "Yea the sparrow hath found a house, and the swallow a nest for herself." It was June 17th, 1722. The first step in the building of Herrnhut was complete. Nevertheless, for many weeks following, this band of settlers had little food, the children fell ill, and many of the neighbors mocked them.

In writing a letter to Zinzendorf, Heitz called this place Herrnhut, or *the watch of the Lord*. It was a name that played on the land's original title, and that came with a double meaning. First it would be a place under the Lord's watchful care; a place of refuge under the canopy of the Lord's presence. Secondly, in this place the Moravians would keep watch before the Lord—in worship, prayer and intercession. A key passage for Zinzendorf and the Moravians was Isaiah 62:6-7, which declares:

> On your walls, O Jerusalem, I have set watchmen; all the day and all the night they shall never be silent. You who put the Lord in remembrance, take no rest, and give him no rest until he establishes Jerusalem and makes it a praise in the earth.

When Zinzendorf returned home on December 2nd, 1722, he saw a light up on the hill, where the first home had been built on his estate. He entered the house, assured these persecuted refugees of his blessing, fell down to his knees, and dedicated the little community to the Lord.

Prayer

Lord, help us to be willing and available to follow You as the Lamb wherever You lead.

Reflection and Bible Study

Luke 9:23 *"And he said to all, 'If anyone would come after me, let him deny himself and take up his cross daily and follow me.'"*

Q. Where do you sense God leading you today? What does it mean in your life to deny yourself, take up your cross daily, and follow Jesus?

Matthew 28:18-20 *"And Jesus came and said to them, 'All authority in heaven and on earth has been given to me. Go therefore and make disciples of all nations, baptizing them in the name of the Father and of the Son and of the Holy Spirit, teaching them to observe all that I have commanded you. And behold, I am with you always, to the end of the age.'"*

Q. Recall the rules of the Order of the Mustard seed: *being true to Christ; being kind to people;* and *taking the gospel to the nations.* In which of these areas, and in what ways, do you want to see spiritual progress in your life?

CHAPTER THREE

Summer of Revival

For the next five years, from 1722 to 1727, the small Moravian community struggled in many ways. They experienced false teaching and prophecy, dissension, bitterness, and judgement against one another.

As the settlement began to grow, word began to spread that the Count had offered his estate as an asylum for persecuted Protestants, prompting all sorts of religious folks to come and make Herrnhut their new home. As J.E. Hutton writes:

> Some had a touch of Calvinism, and were fond of discussing free will and predestination; some were disciples of the sixteenth century Anabaptist mystic, Casper Schwenkfeld; some were vague evangelicals from Swabia; some were Lutheran Pietists from near at hand; and some, such as the 'Five Churchmen,' were descendants of the Brethren's Church and wished to see her revived on German soil. The result was dissension in the camp. As the settle-

ment grew larger, things grew worse. As the settlers learned to know each other better they learned to love each other less. As poverty crept in the door, love flew out the window.[17]

Five years had passed since the first settlers had arrived. When Zinzendorf caught wind of what was now taking place, he moved from Berthelsdorf to Herrnhut in 1727. Zinzendorf was just 27 years of age. He went from home to home, preaching the cross of Christ, and pleading with the young community to forgive one another, practice reconciliation, and grow in love for each other.

On May 12th, 1727, after a lecture by Zinzendorf, members of the community signed a contract called the *Brotherly Agreement* to dedicate their lives to the service of Jesus Christ. It was at this point that the Spirit began to move in a deeper way among them. On July 22nd, the community covenanted to meet often in prayer and worship, beginning what would later be referred to as the 'summer of revival' for this small Moravian community. Zinzendorf remarked that "the whole place represented a visible tabernacle of God among men."[18]

For the next several months, the city on the hill was full of joy, and the very men who had quarreled with each other now formed groups for prayer and praise. The Count held meetings every day, and the Berthelsdorf church was crowded out at every gathering. During the summer months, Bible studies focused on First John, the epistle of love.

The Moravian Pentecost

At the time of the revival in Herrnhut in 1727, there were 220 people living in 30 different homes in Herrnhut, and 87 of them were children. Zinzendorf took the children under his wing, first in Berthelsdorf, and later in Herrnhut. Zinzendorf had a special love for children and youth, since he had experienced God much in his youth. He would spend significant time discipling the children and praying for God's Spirit to fill them.

The answer came first through a small 11-year-old girl named Susanne Kühnel. She had been living in Herrnhut for two years. On May 2nd, her godly mother had died, going home to Jesus with much joy. On August 6th, after Susanne had spent three days in prayer, she was filled with indescribable joy at one in the morning. She awakened her father, who had been a witness to everything, telling him, "Father, now I am a child of God, and now I know how it was and still is with my mother." [19]

Susanne's father went the next morning to the Count and told him what had happened. There, he heard the news that in the same night, three other girls also experienced revival and had wept for grace. The Count called them all to himself, prayed with them and blessed them. Through their testimony, other children were revived as well. These children along with the adults began praying for a mighty move of the Holy Spirit.

Throughout the summer months, the Moravians had come together in unity and one accord, emptying themselves of all idolatry. Now they were ready to receive a fresh infilling of the Holy Spirit.

On August 5th, Zinzendorf and 14 others spent the night in prayer to God.

On August 10th, Pastor Rothe was so overwhelmed by the Holy Spirit that he "sank down to the dust," under conviction of the presence of the Lord. The entire community followed and continued until midnight in prayer, singing and weeping.

At the invitation of Pastor Rothe, on Monday August 13th, 1727, the community walked from Herrnhut to the Lutheran church in Berthelsdorf to celebrate communion. There, Zinzendorf shared a powerful sermon on the cross of Christ and the glory of the Lamb. After further confession of sin, and reconciliation amongst the brethren, they came to the communion table and the Holy Spirit fell upon them. The moment was so powerful that many referred to it as a 'Moravian Pentecost.' As they received the love of God poured out into their hearts by the Holy Spirit, it spilled out in extraordinary love for one another. Some referred to the experience as a "baptism of love." However the event can best be described, the Moravians had obtained the firm conviction that they were one in Christ. In a letter held in the Moravian archives in Herrnhut, it is said that:

> After August 13th, there was such a movement in the fellowship, that the bushes on the Hutberg were filled with brothers, sisters, and children day and night, who on their knees or prostrate, prayed, wept and sang.[20]

From August 13th to 17th, the children prayed until one in the morning on the Hutberg, then went singing through the village to their homes in Berthelsdorf, whereby the mother of one told her daughter, "Be quiet and [do] not cry out so loud. You are waking up the whole area." The archives continue:

> On August 23rd, there was such a spirit of prayer that gripped the boys and girls, that no one could listen to them without being moved to the heart, and there was an extraordinary move in their meetings through Susanne who daily became more faithful and serious. On August 29th from 11pm until 1am in the night, there was heart-moving praying and singing from the girls. At the same time the boys were lying in another place in prayer. It was such a powerful move of the Spirit amongst the children, that words fail to describe it.[21]

The revival amongst the children had a great influence on the parents and the rest of the inhabitants of Herrnhut. I believe it is a lesson for us today that the revival season of the Moravians was intergenerational. Just as in the book of Acts, three generations came together in united prayer that led to a season of Pentecost.

The Brethren commented that they had "learned to love." From that time forward, the Moravian missionary David Nitchsmann said that, "Herrnhut was a living church of Jesus Christ. We thank the Lord that we ever came to Herrnhut."[22]

The words of the Moravian poet James Montgomery sum up this season of revival well:

They walked with God in peace and love
But failed with one another.
While sternly for the faith they strove,
Brother fell out with brother;
But He in whom they put their trust,
Who knew their frames that they were dust,
Pitied and healed their weakness.
He found them in His house of prayer,
With one accord assembled;
And so revealed His presence there,
They wept for joy and trembled;
One cup they drank, one bread they brake,
One baptism shared, one language spake,
Forgiving and forgiven.
Then forth they went, with tongues of flame,
In one blest theme, delighting,
The love of Jesus and His name,
God's children all uniting.[23]

Prayer

Father, we ask that You fill us with Your Holy Spirit today. Show us if there is anyone in our lives who we need to forgive or be reconciled to, and give us the courage to reach out to them with Your love.

Reflection and Bible Study

Ephesians 5:15-18 *"Look carefully then how you walk, not as unwise but as wise, making the best use of the time, because the days are evil. Therefore do not be foolish, but understand what the will of the Lord is. And do not get drunk with wine, for that is debauchery, but be filled with the Spirit…"*

Q. Are you hungry for more of the presence of God in your life? Are you seeking for a fresh encounter with His Spirit? Why or why not?

Ephesians 4:32 *"Be kind to one another, tenderhearted, forgiving one another, as God in Christ forgave you."*

Q. Is there anyone that you need to forgive or be reconciled to? Are there any relationships where you need to see more unity and oneness in Christ?

CHAPTER FOUR

Fire on the Altar

After the outpouring of the Holy Spirit at Herrnhut, the Lord spoke to Zinzendorf from Leviticus 6:13, impressing upon him that the fire should never go out on the altar. As the fire in the Jewish temple was never allowed to burn out, so the community at Herrnhut resolved that the incense of intercessory prayer should rise continually day and night in this new temple of the Lord. They believed that the right response to the sacrifice of Christ and the absolute worth of Jesus was their unceasing prayer.

On August 26th, the Moravians launched a canopy of continual prayer with 24 men and 24 women, committed to an hour of prayer daily. A person would commit to the same hour each day. They called this "hourly intercession," inspired by Christ's exhortation to Peter at Gethsemane, "Could you not watch with me one hour?" (Matthew 26:40). The list included seven names of the revived girls, who were committed to praying one hour a day. Eventually the number of intercessors increased from 48 to 77. Most of them were simple, ordinary believers—housewives, craftsmen, bakers, and children.

This prayer chain of unrivalled commitment swept through the community and ultimately lasted over a hundred years. The Moravians didn't pray in just one location, but as they went about their normal lives in their homes, on walks, and during work breaks. They would often be praying in pairs or triplets during their committed hours of prayer. Their mission statement was "one on the field, one at home, one to pray and one to go."

Not only did this group pray, but they combined prayer with worship and praise. They would gather together in the mornings and evenings to start and end their day in songs of praise.[24] Zinzendorf was a prolific songwriter, writing and composing some 2,000 hymns.

During an evening service on May 3rd, 1728, Zinzendorf gave the community a verse from Scripture; a watchword for the next day. The Moravians who had been at the service took this word to the more than 30 homes in the community and exhorted believers to use this verse for the next day's prayer and worship focus. These 'watchwords' were compiled and eventually published in 1731, one for each day of the year, called the Daily Text.

Zinzendorf would also gather the committed "hourly intercessors" once a week to share prayer points. Prayer was primarily outward and kingdom-focused. Rather than simply praying for individual needs, the intercessors would cry out for other communities; for missionaries on the field; and for the gospel of the kingdom to be proclaimed in power and demonstrated in love.

It was under this canopy of day-and-night prayer that God began to mark missionaries to carry the gospel to the ends of the earth. Zinzendorf's passion for the lost grew hand-in-hand with his passion for Jesus. Equipped with just a handful of saints, a burning love for Jesus and the power of prayer, he made it his determined aim to evangelize the world.

Their newfound missionary zeal was given expression in a seal, which is now universally recognized as the logo of the Moravians. Composed of a lamb on a crimson ground waving the resurrection cross on a triumphal banner, the seal's motto reads, "Our Lamb has conquered; let us follow Him."

Prayer

Lord Jesus, I ask, teach me how to pray. Increase my desire to spend more time with You each day. Help me to become devoted to You in prayer.

Reflection and Bible Study

Colossians 4:2-4 *"Continue steadfastly in prayer, being watchful in it with thanksgiving. At the same time, pray also for us,* *that God may open to us a door for the word, to declare the mystery of Christ, on account of which I am in prison—that I may make it clear, which is how I ought to speak."*

Q. Prayer is the conversational part of the most important love relationship in our lives. What are the barriers that you encounter in your prayer life?

Matthew 26:40 *"And he came to the disciples and found them sleeping. And he said to Peter, 'So, could you not watch with me one hour?'"*

Q. What do you think motivated the Moravians to "keep watch" in hourly intercession each day?

CHAPTER FIVE

Lord of the Harvest

Missions proved to be Zinzendorf's greatest achievement.

Attending the coronation of Christian IV of Denmark in Copenhagen in 1731, Zinzendorf was introduced to a black slave from the Danish West Indies. The slave's name was Anthony Ulrich. Zinzendorf invited Anthony to Herrnhut to share his story. Anthony had a profound impact on the community. A few months later, after an unforgettable service on August 18th, John Leonard Dober, a potter, and David Nitschmann, a carpenter, were commissioned and sent out by the congregation to reach the West Indies slaves with the gospel of Jesus Christ.

On October 8th, 1732, John and David left in a Dutch ship from the Copenhagen harbor, bound for the Danish West Indies. Both men were skilled speakers, and ready to sell themselves into slavery to reach those already bound in the West Indies. As the ship slipped away, John and David let out a passionate declaration that would eventually become the battle cry for all Moravian missionaries: "May the Lamb that was slain receive the reward of His suffering."

The Moravians' passion for souls was surpassed only by their passion for the Lamb of God, Jesus Christ.

The Moravian Missions Movement

When these two men set out in 1732 to take the gospel to the West Indies, William Carey, the "father of Protestant missions," was yet to be born. It would be another 150 years before the missionary pioneer Hudson Taylor would arrive in China. John Leonard Dober and David Nitschmann were the first missionaries sent out by the Moravian community. Within twenty years, Moravian missionaries would be found in the Arctic among the Eskimos, in southern Africa, among the Indians of North America, in Suriname, Ceylon, China, India, Persia, Algeria, Romania, and beyond. Writes Steve Addison:

> By the time other Christian missionaries arrived, fifty years later, the Moravians had baptized 13,000 converts and planted churches on the islands of St. Thomas, St. Croix, Jamaica, Antigua, Barbados and St. Kitts. The Moravians were the first Protestants to treat world missions as the responsibility of the whole church. Under Zinzendorf, the Moravians became an intense and highly mobile missionary movement.[25]

From a community of approximately 500 residents in Herrnhut during the years 1732-1742, some 70 missionaries had already been sent out. As these missionary movements began to
spread, persecution increased, including the banishment of
Count Zinzendorf from Saxony in 1736.

Despite the increasing persecution, another Moravian missionary settlement was established 350 miles to the west in
Herrnhaag. Herrnhaag soon surpassed Herrnhut, sending out
200 missionaries over a two-year period. *Christian History*
magazine reported that "the decade of 1732–1742 stands un-
paralleled in Christian history in so far as missionary expan-
sion is concerned."[26] Moreover, Steve Addison writes that,
"Within two decades the Moravians sent out more missionaries
than all Protestants had sent out in the previous two hundred
years. The rapid deployment of so many young missionaries
around the world was remarkable."[27] Indeed, in the words of
one historical account:

> The Moravians recognized themselves in debt to the world as the
> trustees of the gospel. They were taught to embrace a lifestyle of
> self-denial, sacrifice and prompt obedience. They followed the call
> of the Lamb to go anywhere and with an emphasis upon the worst
> and hardest places as having the first claim. No soldiers of the
> cross have ever been bolder as pioneers, more patient or persis-
> tent in difficulties, more heroic in suffering, or more entirely de-
> voted to Christ and the souls of men than the Moravian Brother-
> hood.[28]

In 1791, an evangelical report published by the Moravians explained their undying motivation for missions:

The simple motive of the brethren for sending missionaries to distant nations was and is an ardent desire to promote the salvation of their fellow men, by making known to them the gospel of our Savior Jesus Christ. It grieved them to hear of so many thousands and millions of the human race sitting in darkness and groaning beneath the yoke of sin and the tyranny of Satan; and remembering the glorious promises given in the Word of God, that the heathen also should be the reward of the sufferings and death of Jesus; and considering His commandment to His followers, to go into all the world and preach the gospel to every creature, they were filled with confident hopes that if they went forth in obedience unto, and believing in His word, their labor would not be in vain in the Lord. They were not dismayed in reflecting on the smallness of their means and abilities, and that they hardly knew their way to the heathen whose salvation they so ardently longed for, nor by the prospect of enduring hardships of every kind and even perhaps the loss of their lives in the attempt. Yet their love to their Savior and their fellow sinners for whom He shed His blood, far outweighed all these considerations. They went forth in the strength of their God and He has wrought wonders in their behalf.[29]

Zinzendorf stated his missionary theory along three lines. First, the missionary was to live humbly among the people and not dominate them. Second, the crucified Christ was to be the focal point of preaching and teaching. Third, the missionaries were not to seek the conversion of whole nations but were to look for the man of peace in a community, and search out for individual seekers. They would disciple men and women, calling them to make disciples worth reproducing.

Part of Zinzendorf's missionary philosophy was called "first fruits." His belief was that the wholesale conversion of the world would have to await the prior conversion of the Jews grafted back into the one new man (cf. Romans 9-11). In the meantime, the gospel would go forth, and many "first fruits" believers would be discipled and churches planted in every nation or people group on the earth.

Prayer

Lord of the Harvest, we ask You to send forth laborers into the harvest fields of the nations. Father, we ask You to give Your Son the nations as His inheritance (Luke 10:2, Psalm 2).

Reflection and Bible Study

Matthew 9:35-38 *"And Jesus went throughout all the cities and villages, teaching in their synagogues and proclaiming the gospel of the kingdom and healing every disease and every affliction. When he saw the crowds, he had compassion for them, because they were harassed and helpless, like sheep without a shepherd. Then he said to his disciples, 'The harvest is plentiful,* *but the laborers are few; therefore pray earnestly to the Lord of the harvest to send out laborers into his harvest."'*

Q. What do you think is God's heart for the nations?

Matthew 28:18-20 *"And Jesus came and said to them, 'All authority in heaven and on earth has been given to me. Go therefore and make disciples of all nations, baptizing them in the name of the Father and of the Son and of the Holy Spirit, teaching them to observe all that I have commanded you. And behold, I am with you always, to the end of the age.'"*

Q. What does it look like for us to make disciples of all nations today?

CHAPTER SIX

Awakening a Giant

The global influence of the 18th century Moravian missionaries can hardly be overstated. One of the key figures from history on whom they had a profound impact was none other than John Wesley. In fact, Wesley's contact with the Moravians led directly to his conversion experience.[30] John Wesley meticulously recorded his observations of and encounters with the Moravians—whom he often called simply "the Germans"—in his journal between the years 1736 and 1738.

Below are reproduced several selections from Wesley's journal that provide an insight into the character and spirit of the Moravian movement, and the impression they left on the founder of the Methodists. In the first, Wesley is on board a ship bound for America, when he observes the Moravians in the face of life-threatening storms.

At seven I went to the Germans. I had long before observed the great seriousness of their behavior. Of their humility, they had given a continual proof, by performing those servile offices for the other passengers, which none of the English would undertake; for which they desired, and would receive no pay, saying, "it was good for their proud hearts," and "their loving Savior had done more for them." And every day had given them occasion of showing a meekness which no injury could move. If they were pushed, struck, or thrown down, they rose again and went away; but no complaint was found in their mouth. There was now an opportunity of trying whether they were delivered from the Spirit of fear, as well as from that of pride, anger, and revenge. In the midst of the psalm wherewith their service began, the sea broke over, split the main-sail in pieces, covered the ship, and poured in between the decks, as if the great deep had already swallowed us up. A terrible screaming began among the English. The Germans calmly sung on. I asked one of them afterwards, "Was you not afraid?" He answered, "I thank God, no." I asked, "But were not your women and children afraid?" He replied, mildly, "No; our women and children are not afraid to die."

From them I went to their crying, trembling neighbours, and pointed out to them the difference in the hour of trial, between him that feareth God, and him that feareth Him not. At twelve the wind fell. This was the most glorious day which I have hitherto seen.

John Wesley was especially attracted and eventually attached to one of the Moravian brothers, Peter Bohler, in England. God used Bohler to show Wesley that although he was an ordained minister, he did not have saving faith in Christ. Although Bohler was much younger than Wesley, Wesley would later refer to him as his spiritual father.

John Wesley's Conversion

On Wednesday May 24th, 1738, John Wesley wrote in his journal, summarizing his life-changing conversion experience:

> In my return to England, January, 1738, being in imminent danger of death, and very uneasy on that account, I was strongly convinced that the cause of that uneasiness was unbelief; and that the gaining a true, living faith was the "one thing needful" for me. But still I fixed not this faith on its right object: I meant only faith in God, not faith in or through Christ. Again, I knew not that I was wholly void of this faith; but only thought, I had not enough of it.
>
> In the evening I went very unwillingly to a society in Aldersgate-Street, where one was reading Luther's preface to the Epistle to the Romans. About a quarter before nine, while he was describing the change which God works in the heart through faith in Christ, I felt my heart strangely warmed. I felt I did trust in Christ, Christ alone for salvation: And an assurance was given me, that He had taken away *my* sins, even *mine*, and saved *me* from the law of sin and death.

John Wesley Visits Herrnhut

On Tuesday August 8th, 1738, Wesley wrote in his journal about his visit to Herrnhut. In this account, he provides invaluable details about daily life there. One incident is particularly vivid and illuminating:

> A child was buried. The burying-ground (called by them Gottes Acker, that is, God's ground) lies a few hundred yards out of the town, under the side of a little wood. There are distinct squares in it for married men and unmarried; for married and unmarried women; for male and female children, and for widows. The corpse was carried from the chapel, the children walking first; next the orphan-father (so they call him who has the chief care of the Orphan house), with the Minister of Berthelsdorf; then four children bearing the corpse; and after them, Martin Dober and the father of the child. Then followed the men; and last of all the women and girls. They all sung as they went. Being come into the square where the male children are buried, the men stood on two sides of it, the boys on the third, and the women and girls on the fourth. There they sung again; after which the Minister used (I think read) a short prayer, and concluded with that blessing, "Unto God's gracious mercy and protection I commit you." Seeing the father (a plain man, a tailor by trade) looking at the grave, I asked, "How do you find yourself?" He said, "Praised be the Lord, never better. He has taken the soul of my child to himself. I have seen, according to my desire, his body committed to holy ground. And I know that when it is raised again, both he and I shall be ever with the Lord."

Moravian Impact on John Wesley

In John Wesley's journal entry dated Saturday August 12th, 1738, he sums up his overall response to Herrnhut:

Today was the Intercession-day, when many strangers were present, some of whom came twenty or thirty miles. I would gladly have spent my life here; but my Master calling me to labor in another part of his vineyard, on *Monday*, 14, I was constrained to take my leave of this happy place; Martin Dober, and a few others of the brethren, walking with us about an hour, O when shall this Christianity cover the earth, as the "waters cover the sea"?

To hear in what manner God "out of darkness commanded this light to shine," must be agreeable to all those in every nation, who can testify from their own experience, "The gracious Lord hath so done His marvelous acts, that they ought to be had in remembrance." I shall therefore here subjoin the substance of several conversations, which I had at Herrnhut, chiefly on this subject. And may many be incited hereby to give praise "unto Him that sitteth upon the throne, and unto the Lamb for ever and ever!"

Several years later, Zinzendorf released twelve Moravian missional communities in England into the hands of John Wesley, whom he recognized had the leadership gifting to plant churches. This helped to serve and establish the Methodist movement in England.

Thus God used Zinzendorf, Peter Bohler and the Moravians in a profound way to impact John Wesley and the Methodist movement.

Prayer

Lord, we praise You for how You work through history, using ordinary people for Your extraordinary purposes. Strangely warm our hearts as you did for John Wesley. Use us to inspire a new generation of missionaries. We surrender ourselves to Your call and purposes.

Reflection and Bible Study

1 Corinthians 15:51-58 *"Behold! I tell you a mystery. We shall not all sleep, but we shall all be changed, in a moment, in the twinkling of an eye, at the last trumpet. For the trumpet will sound, and the dead will be raised imperishable, and we shall be changed. For this perishable body must put on the imperishable, and this mortal body must put on immortality. When the perishable puts on the imperishable, and the mortal puts on immortality, then shall come to pass the saying that is written:*

"Death is swallowed up in victory.

O death, where is your victory?

O death, where is your sting?"

The sting of death is sin, and the power of sin is the law. But thanks be to God, who gives us the victory through our Lord Jesus Christ. Therefore, my beloved brothers, be steadfast, immovable, always abounding in the work of the Lord, knowing that in the Lord your labor is not in vain."

Q. What did the seafaring Moravians understand about death that so struck John Wesley?

Habakkuk 2:14 *"For the earth will be filled with the knowledge of the glory of the Lord as the waters cover the sea."*

Q. Who is your John Wesley? Who can you welcome more closely into your life and invest in for the advancement of God's kingdom?

CHAPTER SEVEN

Let the Nations Be Glad

The Moravians were missionary trailblazers, setting an incredible precedent that has inspired the church for generations. While they took the gospel to many lands, let us briefly consider two of their key missionary enterprises—in South Africa and North America.

The Khoisan in South Africa

In 1737, a young bachelor Moravian missionary by the name of Georg Schmidt was sent to South Africa. The following year, he started the first mission station in southern Africa at Genadendal or *Valley of Grace*, in the Western Cape. Originally the place had been known as Baviaanskloof—*the valley of the baboons.*

Georg Schmidt arrived at a time when the Indigenous people, known as the Khoisan, were suffering from a smallpox epidemic against which they had no immunity. Prior to this, the Khoisan's way of life was already under threat from an influx of European farmers. In the words of one account:

> As a people they were on the verge of extinction and, against enormous odds, Schmidt formed a small congregation and taught the Khoisan to read and write. His good works came unstuck, however, when he began baptizing the converts and the Dutch clergy based in Cape Town threw up their hands in horror. According to them, Schmidt was not an ordained minister and therefore had no right to administer the sacraments. In 1743 Schmidt was forced to return to Europe. The Mission Station was abandoned until almost 50 years later when three Missionaries returned to resume Schmidt's work.[31]

The arrival of this second wave of Moravian missionaries to Genadendal is picked up by another history documenting the Genadendal Mission Station:

> Almost 50 years after Schmidt left, a chance encounter between a Moravian Church member travelling to Europe and a local priest at the Cape set things in motion to re-establish the Moravian mission.
>
> In November 1792, the Moravian headquarters in Europe sent three men to the Cape. Hendrick Marsveld, a 47-year-old tailor, Daniel Schwinn, a 42-year-old shoemaker, and Christian Kühnel, a 30-year-old knife maker.
>
> On arriving at Baviaanskloof, Khoikhoi living in a kraal not far from the mission showed the men where Schmidt's house had been. Some of the walls were still standing. They were also told

that Schmidt had planted an almond, apricot and pear tree. Schmidt had given his classes underneath the pear tree. To this day a pear tree still grows in the original location of Schmidt's one.

The missionaries also met Vehettge Tikkuie who was Schmidt's cook and housekeeper and had been one of the five baptized by him. After being baptized, she took the name Magdelena. Before he left, Schmidt gave her a copy of the New Testament and asked her to take care of his flock while he was away.

For nearly 50 years Magdelena continued preaching and teaching others to read the Bible and pray. She did so under the same pear tree which Schmidt had used. She still had the copy of the New Testament that had been given to her by Schmidt. The book is now kept at the Genadendal Mission Museum.

Magdelena told them that when Schmidt left, the converts returned to working at the farms and many of them had since died. Life had steadily gotten worse for the Khoi, who according to Magdelena, were not as poor as they were 'now.' When the missionaries told Lena that they had come to continue the work in Baviaanskloof, her response was, 'Thanks be to God.' Magdelena continued to help at the mission until her death on 3 January 1800.[32]

In 1818, the colonial government of South Africa asked the Moravians to take over the pastoral care of patients at the recently finished hospital in Hemel en Aarde. This is when they began their work among leprosy patients. The Moravian missionaries knew that these precious souls who had leprosy needed both a human touch and a divine touch, even if it might cost the missionaries their lives.

By 1845, the South African government decided to close the hospital and move patients to a more isolated location on Robben Island. This prompted the patients to petition the government for the Moravian missionaries to join them in the move. So in January of 1846, Moravian missionaries Joseph and Friederike Lehmann arrived at the General Infirmary on Robben Island, and continued their work among the leprosy patients. One Moravian source records the warm welcome the Lehmanns received:

> The whole company of lepers broke forth in songs of praise to the Lord, for sending these missionaries who had brought restoration, hope and healing to them through the gospel of Jesus Christ![33]

The Native Indians in North America

Burdened to reach the Native Americans, Zinzendorf moved to America to help establish a few missionary settlements from 1741 to 1743. He founded the towns of Bethlehem and Nazareth in Pennsylvania, and Salem in North Carolina. It was reported during a Christmas Eve service that Zinzendorf named the first town Bethlehem in light of the Christmas story. Moravian missionary John Martin Mack wrote:

> Thus the new place was named Bethlehem. I still remember the impression I had during it all and I will keep it until I die. And so, he named the new settlement Bethlehem.[34]

Zinzendorf helped begin churches in major cities such as Philadelphia and New York. His daughter Benigna founded one of the earliest schools for girls in the country. The American Indians called the elder Zinzendorf "Johanan", meaning *blessed through grace.*

When Zinzendorf and his travel company sailed back to England in January of 1743, his followers continued the work. They founded a settlement in Moravian Falls, North Carolina, established 24/7 prayer, and also reached out to the neighboring Cherokee Indians with the love of Jesus. In North Carolina, the Cherokee Indians were forced to move out from Georgia to Indian Territory in 1838, walking what would later be called the Trail of Tears.

The Trail of Tears was a series of forced displacements of around 60,000 Native American Indians. The territory to which they were forcibly displaced was in present-day Oklahoma. From these events, the Cherokee knew for sure that they had no real protection from the U.S. Constitution. Many of the Moravian missionaries left their homes to walk the Trail of Tears with their friends, the Cherokee Indians. Although along this tragic journey, more than 4,000 Cherokees died from the hard conditions they faced, hundreds gave their lives to Christ, having seen the powerful witness of the Moravian missionaries' sacrificial love.

The Moravians left an unmistaken and indelible mark on the culture of early America.

The Moravian Diaspora

The Moravians loved the whole church and were often referred to as the "church within the church". Zinzendorf encouraged the Moravian believers to stay connected to the Lutheran church in Germany and yet maintain their pietistic gatherings and small missional communities. The goal for Zinzendorf and his friend Christian David was to form "little churches within the church"—to act as a leaven, revitalizing and unifying churches into one communion.

Many Moravians went to cities throughout Europe to come alongside the church and make disciples worth reproducing. This became known as the Moravian Diaspora. An example of their discipling influence was in how they helped shape the life of Dietrich Bonhoeffer. Two Moravian sisters, Kathe and Maria Van Horn, came to live with the Bonhoeffers after Dietrich was born. For two decades, they formed a vital part of the Bonhoeffer family's discipleship to Jesus, watching and educating the children.

Count Zinzendorf's life was far from flawless. But his burning love for Jesus Christ was unquestionable, a glimpse of which can be seen in the following letter he wrote:

> Our method of proclaiming salvation is this: to point out to every heart the loving Lamb, who died for us, and although He was the Son of God, offered Himself for our sins [...] by the preaching of His blood, and of His love unto death, even the death of the cross, never, either in discourse or in argument, to digress even for a

quarter of an hour from the loving Lamb: to name no virtue except in Him, and from Him and on His account; to preach no commandment except faith in Him, no other justification but that He atoned for us, no other sanctification but the privilege to sin no more, no other happiness but to be near Him, to think of Him and do His pleasure; no other self-denial but to be deprived of Him and His blessings; no other calamity but to displease Him; no other life but in Him.[35]

When the Moravians celebrated their Jubilee in 1782, it was reported that 165 missionaries from Herrnhut had spread across the earth as far as the Arctic, the Tropics, the Far East and America. Missions endeavors multiplied and continued under the banner of 24/7 worshipful prayer. In total, 226 missionaries were scattered around the world by this time. Each of them were 'tent-making' missionaries, serving communities first with their trade and by working among the people. It is estimated that these missionaries, together with those they discipled and sent out, helped to establish over 5,000 missionary settlements across the globe.

The radical devotion and consecration of these missionaries is astounding. Often they would build their own wooden caskets knowing they wouldn't be returning. Before departing, some missionary families would hold memorial services in the graveyard, understanding they would give their lives for the sake of the gospel.

Over 6,000 people are buried in the graveyard just below the Hutberg. The graveyard is known as "Gottes Acker", an ancient designation for a burial ground which means *Field of God*. Each of the gravestones are flat and simple, communicating the truth that all God's people are equal before the foot of the cross. Apparently, the first sunrise service was launched in 1732 by a group of single Moravian brothers. The Herrnhut diary records:

> We agreed among our band of young men that this Easter morning we were to go up the Hutberg early before the rise of the sun. This happened [...] early before 4 o'clock. After we had spent 1 1/2 hours with singing we returned to have a prayer meeting, during which we sang several hymns and read the third chapter of Peter's first letter.[36]

It seems that Zinzendorf was also present that morning. "This morning we had the nicest celebration among our graves," he later wrote in a letter to his cousin Ludwig von Castell.

Ring the Bell of Awakening

The Moravian movement had provided leadership to the world for 200 years. But by the 1930s and 40s, sadly the town of Herrnhut had followed the rest of Germany in providing tacit—if not eager—support for Adolf Hitler's Nazi party. The Soviet Army captured the town of Herrnhut on the final day of the Second World War, at which time the church building and the heart of the town were set ablaze. It was a scene that caused locals to wonder if this was the Lord's judgment.

The only edifice in Herrnhut still standing after the flames went out was the church courtyard's bell tower. Every other wall of the church was at least partly destroyed, but miraculously, the bell tower remained intact. Steve Thompson writes:

> The Herrnhut congregation originally owned three bells, that [...] were surrendered to the Nazi party for the German war machine during previous years. Immediately after the war ended, congregations across Germany began searching for bells to fill their belfries. Amazingly, a Moravian congregation in northern Germany located the only remaining bell from Herrnhut not melted down for military use. The bell's authenticity was confirmed because it contained a quotation that Zinzendorf had inscribed on it.
>
> After two years, this bell was returned to the Herrnhut bell tower. We were stunned to learn that the stanza on the bell read, "Herrnhut should only continue as long as the purposes of God go forth unhindered." That the bell tower was the only structure left intact reveals that God wanted this message to sound as clear as a bell to future generations. When the purposes of God ceased to go forth unhindered, Herrnhut ceased to exist.[37]

May all of us hear and surrender to the purposes of the Lord in these days. May we return and walk in "the fear of the Lord."

As the Bride of Christ, we are in need today of genuine, heartfelt repentance. Jesus, our worthy Bridegroom, cries out to us as He did to the church at Ephesus:

> Nevertheless, I have this against you, that you have left your first love. Remember therefore from where you have fallen; repent and do the first works. (Revelation 2:4-5)[38]

Like the Moravians, we need to return to our first love, to the Lord Jesus, our Lamb of love. We need to ask Him to ring the bell of awakening in these days. Let us cry out for a Lamb's awakening movement, where the Spirit of God uses the Word of God to reawaken the people of God to the Lamb of God for all that He is!

Prayer

Father, I ask You to give me a burden for the lost and broken. As Isaiah cried out in Isaiah 6:8, "Here I am Lord, Send Me!"

Reflection and Bible Study

Isaiah 6:1-8 *"In the year that King Uzziah died I saw the Lord sitting upon a throne, high and lifted up; and the train of his robe filled the temple. Above him stood the seraphim. Each had six wings: with two he covered his face, and with two he covered his feet, and with two he flew. And one called to another and said: 'Holy, holy, holy is the Lord of hosts; the whole earth is full of his glory!'*

And the foundations of the thresholds shook at the voice of him who called, and the house was filled with smoke. And I said: 'Woe is me! For I am lost; for I am a man of unclean lips, and I dwell in the midst of a people of unclean lips; for my eyes have seen the King, the Lord of hosts!'

Then one of the seraphim flew to me, having in his hand a burning coal that he had taken with tongs from the altar. And he touched my mouth and said: 'Behold, this has touched your lips; your guilt is taken away, and your sin atoned for.'

And I heard the voice of the Lord saying, 'Whom shall I send, and who will go for us?' Then I said, 'Here I am! Send me.'"

Q. What were the key components of the Moravian missions movement?

Revelation 2:4-5 *"But I have this against you, that you have abandoned the love you had at first. Remember therefore from where you have fallen; repent, and do the works you did at first. If not, I will come to you and remove your lampstand from its place, unless you repent."*

Q. What does it look like to return to Jesus as our first love?

CHAPTER EIGHT

Five Marks of the Moravians

The source of the Moravians' success was bound up in their allegiance to and love for Jesus Christ. Because of their love for the Savior, the Moravians experienced a deep sense of community. They maintained this sense of community through small groups based on common needs and interests, original and unifying hymns, continual prayer meetings, fervent preaching of the Word of God, and boasting only in the cross of Christ. The outcome was a massive missionary thrust to the ends of the earth with the gospel.

Consider five marks of the Moravians that can help shape and form us as God's people today.

1. Strategic Missions

The Moravians were the first Protestants to treat world missions as the responsibility of the whole church. Every member was to be on mission, whether at home or abroad. Every member was to be devoted to prayer (cf. Colossians 4:2, Romans 12:12), pleading to the Lord of the Harvest to send forth laborers into the harvest fields of the world, asking the Father to give his Son the nations as His inheritance (cf. Psalm 2:8).

According to Zinzendorf, the command to make disciples of all nations was for every believer. He wrote that, "Missions, after all, is simply this: Every heart with Christ is a missionary, every heart without Christ is a mission field." Moreover, Zinzendorf confessed:

> I have but one passion—it is He, it is He alone. The world is the field and the field is the world; and henceforth that country shall be my home where I can be most used in winning souls for Christ."

It has been noted by missiologists that there are approximately two billion Christians in the world today, with over five billion who don't know Christ. If Jesus were to return today, five billion souls would enter a Christless eternity in hell, suffering with pain, weeping and gnashing of teeth.

In order to grasp the number five billion, picture people standing toe to toe from where you live wrapping all the way around the globe 37 times. It is staggering to consider. These are real people with real stories. *Here I am Lord, send me.* (Isaiah 6:8).

I believe John Stott summarizes well the Moravian call to strategic missions that we must recover today, when he writes, "We must be global Christians, with a global vision because our God is a global God."

I would add that this global vision is all about the global glory of God!

2. Unceasing Prayer and Worship

The Moravians understood that right now, Jesus is being adored with unceasing worship and prayer (cf. Revelation 5:8-9, 8:1-4). If this is the pattern of worship and prayer in heaven, so let this be our pattern on the earth. Jesus is worthy of all of our worship, all of our obedience and all of our affections. Our worship and prayer must be around the throne, around the clock and around the globe.

One of the clearest commands to continual day-and-night, worship-saturated prayer is given to the church at Thessalonica, where Paul writes, "Rejoice always, pray without ceasing, in everything give thanks; for this is the will of God in Christ Jesus for you" (1 Thessalonians 5:16-18).

Paul is asking the church to develop a lifestyle of unceasing, joy-filled thanksgiving and prayer. It is clear that this command is to the gathered church at Thessalonica. As with most commands to pray in the New Testament, Paul is not simply commanding each individual to engage in unceasing prayer. Rather, he is exhorting the corporate body to this lifestyle. He is saying *you all* rejoice, pray and give thanks, for this is God's will for *you all* in Christ Jesus. He is asking them corporately to pray without ceasing, combined with joy-filled thanksgiving, always and in everything.

May this continual, unceasing prayer be saturated with God-exalting worship and praise. As the author of Hebrews reminds us, "Through him then let us continually offer up a sacrifice of praise to God, that is, the fruit of lips that acknowledge his name." (Hebrews 13:15).

Following the Moravians' example, what could it look like today to see canopies of prayer and worship in our churches and cities?

Practically speaking, what if each house church in a city committed to a 24-hour day of enjoyable, thankful prayer once a month, or maybe once a week—and then passed the baton on to the next church in the city? If you had seven churches commit to this one day a week, you would have a canopy of united, strategic and sustainable 24/7 worship-saturated prayer over your city. A similar result could be achieved if you had 30 churches that committed to a 24-hour day of prayer once a month, every month, and people signed up to pray for committed hours of prayer on their particular day. People could commit to convenient times and locations of prayer that fit their busy schedules. Families could commit to praying and worshipping together in their homes. People could also gather together in their churches or in a city-wide house of prayer or prayer tower. Another option would be to pray together with set times over a digital platform like Zoom. It doesn't matter how you organize this. It is simply the principle of churches in your area committing to regular times of worship-saturated prayer around the throne, around the clock and around the globe.

3. Humility and Hiddenness

I have often marveled why most people are not familiar with the story of the Moravians. I believe one of the reasons is that God has kept them and their story hidden. Zinzendorf captured it well when he wrote of himself,

> Remember, you must never use your position to lord it over the heathen. Instead, you must humble yourself and earn their respect through your own quiet faith and the power of the Holy Spirit. The missionary must seek nothing for himself, no seat of honor or hope of fame [...] You must be content to suffer, to die, and to be forgotten.

Isaiah declares that our God dwells in a high and holy place, but also with he who is humble and contrite in spirit (Isaiah 57:15). The Moravians understood their need of a Savior, that they could do nothing apart from Jesus. As Jesus said, "Blessed are the poor in spirit, for theirs is the kingdom of heaven." (Matthew 5:3).

May we grow in deep humility and dependence on God, with a Moravian-like understanding that we are bankrupt apart from Christ. In the words of Zinzendorf, "I am, as ever, a poor sinner, a captive of eternal love, running by the side of His triumphal chariot, and I have no desire to be anything else as long as I live."

God gives grace to the humble, and this simple Moravian community abounded in the grace of God. We know that the essence of gospel humility is, as Pastor Timothy Keller puts it, not thinking more of myself or thinking less of myself: it is *thinking of myself less*. May we be so consumed with the supremacy and glory of Jesus, that He would increase and we would decrease, humbly serving others to the glory of God.

How do we cultivate humility and hiddenness? I believe it is by meditating on the cross. Before we can see what the cross has done for us, we have to see it as something done by us. As John Stott writes, "It is there at the foot of the cross that we shrink to our true size."

In our Bible reading and our life of prayer and worship, we must consistently preach the gospel to ourselves. When we think about what the gospel is, we must always remember that we are not saved by what we do, but completely and fully by what God has done. We are saved wholly by God alone. We do not contribute to our salvation at all.

How can that be? When Jesus Christ came, He lived a life we should have lived and died a death we should have died. He lived a perfect life—in fact, He was the only human being who ever lived a perfect life, and therefore earned God's blessing. At the end of his earthly life, Jesus went to the cross and took the curse that we deserved. When we put our faith in Him, all of our sins and the punishment we deserve fell on Him, and all of the blessing that Jesus deserved came to us. God now treats you and me as though we have done everything that Jesus Christ has done. That is radically good news! Praise be to God.

4. Love for One Another

The Moravians lived out Zinzendorf's famous quote, that "there can be no Christianity without community." One of the primary life verses for Moravian families was John 13:34-35, which says:

> A new commandment I give to you, that you love one another: just as I have loved you, you also are to love one another. By this all people will know that you are my disciples, if you have love for one another.

One of the clearest marks of a disciple of Jesus is love! Scripture makes it abundantly clear that we love because He first loved us. The greatest love ever given was through Jesus at the cross. "Greater love has no one than this, that someone lay down his life for his friends," we read in John 15:13. The Scriptures declare that Jesus loved us and gave himself up for us (cf. Galatians 2:20; Ephesians 5:2, 25; Revelation 1:5). Romans 5:8

says that "God shows his love for us in that while we were still sinners, Christ died for us." In the words of 1 John 4:9-10:

> In this the love of God was made manifest among us, that God sent his only Son into the world, so that we might live through him. In this is love, not that we have loved God but that he loved us and sent his Son to be the propitiation for our sins. Beloved, if God so loved us, we also ought to love one another.

We can only love to the degree that we experience and receive God's love. God desires that the first commandment to love God with our whole heart, mind, soul and strength be restored to first place in our lives. We love God because He first loves us with His whole heart, mind, soul and strength, which He showed us at the cross. When we understand and experience this kind of committed love, revealed through the cross of Christ, we can then love like He loves, laying down our lives for all those around us, and showing ourselves to be His disciples. As we eat His flesh and drink His blood, we abide in Him and He in us. Jesus said in John 6:55-56, "For my flesh is true food, and my blood is true drink. Whoever feeds on my flesh and drinks my blood abides in me, and I in him." As John Stott writes, "the Cross is the blazing fire at which the flame of our love is kindled, but we have to get near enough for its sparks to fall on us."

As the Moravians continually celebrated communion, and meditated on the cross as a lifestyle, they were able to maintain the baptism of love that they experienced at their Moravian

Pentecost. The Moravian movement was a Spirit-led movement, where the love of God was shed abroad in their hearts by the Spirit of God (cf. Romans 5:5).

5. Beholding the Lamb

Zinzendorf was quoted as saying, "I have been bought at a price. I will live every moment of this day so that the Great Purchaser of my soul will receive the full reward of His suffering." It is our desire to see a massive Lamb's awakening movement erupt in our day, where the Spirit of God uses the Word of God to reawaken God's people back to God's Son as the Lamb of all glory!

I believe one of the keys that God will use to unlock the hearts of His people is the revelation of the cross of Christ. In the contemplation of the cross, there is a profound revelation of the love of God. This disclosure comes to the hearts of those who desire to understand this pivotal point in human history. The cross is a wellspring of extravagant love that awaits the seeker who will linger at the foot of the cross long enough with an open and expectant heart. This revelation is given to all who seek God with a whole heart, and whose desire is accompanied by a measure of determination. Consider these powerful declarations of the apostle Paul:

> For I resolved to know nothing while I was with you except Jesus Christ and him crucified. (1 Corinthians 2:2).

May I never boast except in the cross of our Lord Jesus Christ, through which the world has been crucified to me, and I to the world. (Galatians 6:14).

For Christ did not send me to baptize, but to preach the gospel—not with words of human wisdom, lest the cross of Christ be emptied of its power. For the message of the cross is foolishness to those who are perishing, but to us who are being saved it is the power of God. (1 Corinthians 1:17-18).

The cross is both the power of God and the wisdom of God. It is the cross of Christ that brings down all barriers and unites us together in love for His glory. As Jesus said, "But I, when I am lifted up from the earth, will draw all men to myself." (John 12:32). John explains that Jesus said this "to show the kind of death he was going to die." (John 12:33). We also read in Revelation 21:23 that "the city has no need of sun or moon to shine on it, for the glory of God gives it light, and its lamp is the Lamb."

I believe it is time for the church to return to Christ as the Lamb of Love; the Lamb of Glory. As we approach the end of the age, we must see and encounter the face of Jesus as the Lamb!

Twenty-eight times in the book of Revelation, Jesus is revealed as the worthy Lamb! We need to bury our hearts in His wounds until our lives are transformed from glory to glory, for indeed, *every wound bleeds glory*.

When Jesus died, a centurion took a spear and pierced His side. Out of the riven side of the Passover Lamb flowed forth

blood and water. It was a physical sign that His heart had rup-
tured. Jesus' heart was so full of love that it burst open, both in
the natural and in the spiritual. Jesus literally died of a broken
heart!

Out of His heart flowed forth a river of God's love for you and
me. The crimson blood of the Lamb washes away our sin and
makes us whiter than snow. His love was so strong that even
the grave couldn't hold Him back. On the third day, Jesus rose
again and burst forth from the grave, alive forevermore!

It is time to behold the Lamb of Glory until our hearts are
wounded by the Wounded One! As C.H. Spurgeon writes,
"When we see the Lord pierced, the piercing of our hearts be-
gins."

Could the Holy Spirit be holding back the coming wave of
glory until we are gripped with a passion for the Lamb, the One
from whom glory flows? Maybe God is waiting for our hearts to
be scarred by the sacrifice of His Son as the Lamb?

Prayer

*Father, we believe that the hour has come for Your Son, the Lord
Jesus, to be honored and treasured as the worthy Lamb who was
slain. Even as the Lamb is in the center of the throne in Heaven,
we declare and decree that it is time for the Lamb to become the
center of the throne on the earth!*

*Father, we know that you are always looking at the wounds of
your Son. We ask for a Lamb's Reformation in the church that*

would wake us up again to His cross, to bring your Son the reward He deserves for giving His life as a Lamb!

Jesus, You still bear the scars and marks from the cross on Your glorified body in heaven. You stand as a Lamb as though slain. Your scars are medals of glory.

Jesus, You went from wearing a cruel crown of thorns to wearing a golden crown of glory; from robes dipped in blood to a kingly robe of splendor; from a mock scepter in Your hand to a scepter of authority; from the insults of men to the worship of angels; from the filth of sin to the beauty of holiness.

We see Your head and hair, once soaked in blood, now dazzling white as snow. We see Your eyes, stung and dripping blood and tears of sorrow, now blazing like fire, like flaming torches. We see Your face, once swollen and raw from patches of Your beard torn out, now shining brighter than the sun in all its brilliance. We see Your body, once stripped naked, now clothed in eternal majesty. We see Your hands once pierced, now bleeding infinite splendor. We see Your feet once spiked to a stake of timber, now gleaming like burnished bronze. We see Your side, once pierced, and now we hear You say, "This wound in My heart is for you!"

Every wound bleeds glory.

From victim to Victor, from worm to Warrior, from humiliation to glorification, from tortured to triumphant, from degradation to exaltation, from a lowly bleeding sheep, to a glorified Lion-Lamb!

You are the One from whom glory flows! Glory flows from You and through You and back to You!

Lord of the Harvest, would You raise up and send forth messengers of the Lamb, prophetic voices like John the Baptist, who will cry out, "Behold the Lamb of God who takes away the sin of the world."

Would You bring forth ones like Peter who will preach the gospel with such power that people will be cut to the heart, and say, "What must I do to be saved?"

Would You send forth ones like the apostle Paul who will resolve to know nothing but Jesus Christ and Him crucified.

Would You raise up ones like John the apostle who will look until they see the slain Lamb standing in the center of the throne in heaven, and then reveal Him here on the earth!

Would You thrust forth ones like the Moravians who cried out, "May the Lamb who was slain receive the reward for His suffering!"

Reflection and Bible Study

Revelation 5:12 *"Then I looked, and I heard around the throne and the living creatures and the elders the voice of many angels, numbering myriads of myriads and thousands of thousands, saying with a loud voice, 'Worthy is the Lamb who was slain, to receive power and wealth and wisdom and might and honor and glory and blessing!'"*

Q. What makes Jesus worthy and all-deserving of all of our worship, all of our obedience, and all of our affections?

Revelation 21:22-26 *"And I saw no temple in the city, for its temple is the Lord God the Almighty and the Lamb. And the city has no need of sun or moon to shine on it, for the glory of God gives it light, and its lamp is the Lamb. By its light will the nations walk, and the kings of the earth will bring their glory into it, and its gates will never be shut by day—and there will be no night there. They will bring into it the glory and the honor of the nations."*

Q. Recall again the five marks of the Moravians: strategic missions, 24/7 prayer, humility and hiddenness, love for one another, and beholding the Lamb. Which one impacts you most and why?

About the Author

By the grace of God, Jason's desire is be an extravagant worshipper of Jesus, an anointed deliverer of men, and a godly husband and father. Jason has been married for 28 years to Kristie. Together, they have three beautiful children: Jasmine, married to Tyler; Gracelyn; and Joshua. They also have four young grandchildren: Lilly, Abby, Jenna Joy, and Lizzie.

Jason worked as the Associate Pastor of Prayer and Bible at Christ the King Church in Bellingham, Washington, from 2000 to 2010. He completed his Doctorate in Discipleship in 2013 at Talbot Seminary.

From 2008 to 2020, Jason worked as the executive director of Light of the World Prayer Center. The mission statement of Light of the World Prayer Center is to "Exalt Jesus through united, day and night, prayer, praise and worship for Global Harvest."

From 2020 to 2021, Jason served as the Campus Pastor and Adjunct Professor at Arizona Christian University. The mission of ACU is to "Transform Culture with Biblical Truth." During his time at ACU, the university launched a 24/7 Campus Prayer Room.

Jason currently serves as the Executive Coordinator of International Prayer Connect. IPC consists of 25 leaders of significant regional and international prayer networks and ministries throughout the world. The Council seeks to provide relational, prophetic leadership and connection for International

Prayer Connect, a global network of hundreds of prayer networks and ministries with many thousands of ministry leaders and intercessors. IPC's vision is to "Catalyze united prayer across nations, denominations, movements, and generations for the fulfilment of the great commission."

IPC also helps to mobilize prayer for several mission organizations, including Go Movement, GACX, RUN ministries, and Finishing the Task (FTT). In January 2021, IPC launched a global family 24/7 prayer room over a Zoom platform, with 55 nations and 20 languages participating.

Jason also serves as a board member on three other prayer ministries: America Prays, the National Prayer Committee, and Greater Commission Coalition.

Dr Jason Hubbard is on Facebook, Instagram and YouTube, and can be contacted at jason.hubbard@ipcprayer.org.

For International Orders

www.moravianmiracle.org

Price: US$12 (plus postage) with discounts for bulk orders. Also available on Amazon and other digital platforms, both in print and in ebook format. International Prayer Connect (IPC) believes that *Moravian Miracle: The 100 Year Prayer Meeting that Changed the World* is a very important book. It will inspire prayer warriors and multiply prayer in the nations so that "the Lamb who was slain might receive the reward for His suffering." *Moravian Miracle* can be used as an eight-week devotional Bible study and prayer guide. It is a great missional resource for the whole church. IPC is helping distribute *Moravian Miracle* free of charge on a donation basis with suggested prices on their website. International postage can be expensive, so outside of the USA, postage will have to be paid. All donations will help us get more books out and reimburse the author, Dr Jason Hubbard, who is living by faith as a missionary of prayer to the nations and is worthy of our support.

For Australian Orders

www.canberradeclaration.org.au/resources/moravian-miracle

Price AU$18 (plus postage) with discounts for bulk orders. Also available on Amazon and other digital platforms, both in print and in ebook format. The publisher of *Moravian Miracle: The 100 Year Prayer*

Meeting that Changed the World is Australian Heart Publishing. We are a small missions-based publishing ministry established in Australia, and we believe that *Moravian Miracle* is a must-read book for every believer. It will revolutionize prayer warriors and multiply prayer in the nations so that "the Lamb who was slain might receive the reward for His suffering." *Moravian Miracle* can be used as an eight-week devotional Bible study and prayer guide. It is a great missional resource for the whole church. Australian Heart Publishing (through the Canberra Declaration) is giving away these books free of charge on a donation basis with suggested prices on the order form on their website. Sales are only within Australia. All donations will help us get more books out and reimburse the author, Dr Jason Hubbard, who is living by faith as a missionary of prayer to the nations and is worthy of our support.

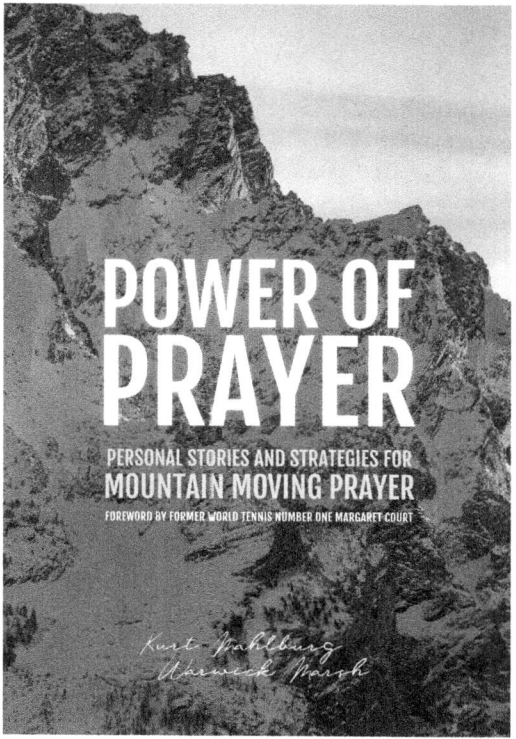

What happens when people pray? In these pages, read the stories of almost one hundred Australians who did, and who saw God answer. Weaving miraculous testimonies with practical teaching, *Power of Prayer* will inspire you to a deeper walk with God, determination in your waiting, and faith that moves even the biggest mountains.

Professionals need not apply. All that's required to be a witness for Jesus is a willing heart. In this book, Kurt and Warwick provide a simple but profound summary of the gospel. Read their personal stories and discover how it's possible for anyone to change the world by sharing the good news of Jesus.

This book was born out of Canberra Declaration's involvement with the GO Movement, an initiative aimed at activating believers to pray and share their faith during May each year. *Power of the Gospel* is warm and readable, and full of real-life stories that will equip you to share your faith in simple and powerful ways. Read the book... pass it on... let's go!

In 2020, the Canberra Declaration marked its 10th anniversary by publishing *The Blessing of Almighty God: The Canberra Declaration Story and the Call to Revitalise Australia.* This book recounts the forging of the landmark Canberra Declaration document and tells the story of those advancing its cause still today.

Australia has taken a huge risk by cutting our culture from its Christian roots. The effects of this are clear to see with the natural family, religious freedom and the sanctity of life withering before us. The Canberra Declaration was written to call Australia back to its Judeo-Christian foundations, so that our way of life can thrive once more.

Our civilization is unstable. Everyone can feel it. We face a looming mental health crisis. Slavery, censorship and superstition are back. Our politics are polarizing. All the affluence in the world can't seem to quench our thirst for meaning and purpose. But maybe there is hope—if we know where to look.

In this timely book, Kurt Mahlburg shows how profoundly the West has been shaped by the life and teachings of Jesus—from our democratic freedoms and our pursuit of reason and science to our belief that every life is precious. Could rediscovering Jesus be the answer to our crisis?

Some have heard about the Moravians, but even less have heard about Count Zinzendorf. He was a man of prayer; a man who could preach all day without tiring. He was an itinerant vagabond for Christ. He urged the Moravians to pray unceasingly, and they prayed unremittingly for over a hundred years.

He wrote that he himself was not so much a God-fearing, but a God-joyful person. Even in his early youth he developed an intimacy with the Lamb of God through prayer. This is a story of persecution, of dissension, of Spirit-filled boldness, of daring enterprises, of dying on mission fields and of congenial relations among the brethren.

NOTES

[1] Rick Joyner, "Father of the Reformation: The Greatest Christian Life," *Morning-Star*, accessed April 21, 2022, https://publications.morningstarministries.org/word-for-the-week/father-reformation-greatest-christian-life.

[2] Justin Holcomb, "The Five Solas: Points from the Past that Should Matter to You," Christianity.com, accessed April 24, 2022, https://www.christianity.com/church/church-history/the-five-solas-of-the-protestant-reformation.html.

[3] Michael Reeves, *The Unquenchable Flame: Discovering the Heart of the Reformation* (Nashville: B&H Publishing Group, 2010), 30.

[4] Rick Joyner, "Father of the Reformation: The Greatest Christian Life," *Morning-Star*, accessed April 21, 2022, https://publications.morningstarministries.org/word-for-the-week/father-reformation-greatest-christian-life.

[5] John Fox, *Fox's Book of Martyrs* (Philadelphia: E. Claxton & Company, 1881), 169-170.

[6] John Fox, *Fox's Book of Martyrs*, 170.

[7] Jesus-Haus Herrnhut, "1628: The Hidden Seed," accessed April 24, 2022, https://www.jh-herrnhut.de/history/.

[8] A.J. Lewis, *Zinzendorf the Ecumenical Pioneer: A Study in the Moravian Contribution to Christian Mission and Unity* (London: SCM Press, 1962), 23.

[9] Sandy Davis Kirk. *The Glory of the Lamb* (Hagerstown: McDougal Publishing Company, 2004), 127.

[10] The Traveling Team, "Count Zinzendorf & The Moravians: Prayer Makes History," accessed April 21, 2022, http://www.thetravelingteam.org/articles/count-zinzendorf-the-moravians-prayer-makes-history.

[11] The Order of the Mustard Seed had no connection to masonic orders.

[12] In Zinzendorf's Footsteps, "Zinzendorf's Life," accessed April 21, 2022, https://zinzendorf.webs.com/zinzendorf-s-life.

[13] Count Zinzendorf, Christian Biography, "Zinzendorf's Wife, Erdmuth Dorothea Von Reuss," accessed April 24, 2022, http://zinzendorf.ccws.org/zinzendorf_contents/zinzendorf_wife.html.

[14] J.E. Hutton, *A History of the Moravian Church* (Pennsylvania: Moravian Publication Office, 1895), 119.

[15] J.E. Hutton, *A History of the Moravian Church*, 69.

[16] Ibid, 69.

[17] Ibid, 72.

[18] Ibid, 73.

[19] Letter held in the Moravian archives, Herrnhut.

[20] Ibid.

[21] Ibid.

[22] J.E. Hutton, *A History of the Moravian Church*, 74.

[23] Ibid, 74.

[24] E.D. Burns, "Moravian Missionary Piety and the Influence of Count Zinzendorf," *Training Leaders International*, accessed April 21, 2022, https://training-leadersinternational.org/jgc/27/moravian-missionary-piety-and-the-influence-of-count-zinzendorf.

[25] Steve Addison, "Stop Sending [uneducated, unordained] Missionaries," *Movements*, accessed April 24, 2022, https://www.movements.net/blog/2016/09/28/requirements-for-missionaries-in-bygone-days.html.

[26] Christianity Today, "The Moravians: Christian History Timeline," accessed April 21, 2022, https://www.christianitytoday.com/history/issues/issue-1/moravians-christian-history-timeline.html.

[27] Steve Addison, *Movements*.

[28] The Traveling Team, "Count Zinzendorf & The Moravians: Prayer Makes History," accessed April 21, 2022, http://www.thetravelingteam.org/articles/count-zinzendorf-the-moravians-prayer-makes-history.

[29] The Traveling Team, "Count Zinzendorf & The Moravians: Prayer Makes History."

[30] Christianity Today, "The Moravians and John Wesley," accessed April 21, 2022, https://www.christianitytoday.com/history/issues/issue-1/moravians-and-john-wesley.html.

[31] South African History Online, "Genadendal Historic Village and Museum," accessed May 4, 2022, https://www.sahistory.org.za/place/genadendal-historic-village-museum.

[32] Genadendal, "The Genadendal Mission Station," accessed April 21, 2022, https://www.genadendal.info/genadendal-mission-station/.

[33] Moravian Archives, "This Month in Moravian History: Moravians on Robben Island," Issue 84, December 2013, http://www.moravianchurcharchives.org/thismonth/13_12%20Robben%20Island.pdf.

[34] Nicole Radzievich, "The man who wrote the story behind Bethlehem's christening," *The Morning Call*, accessed April 21, 2022, https://www.mcall.com/news/local/bethlehem/mc-bethlehem-275th-anniversary-christmas-eve-20161223-story.html.

[35] The Traveling Team, "Count Zinzendorf & The Moravians: Prayer Makes History."

[36] Ibid.

[37] Steve Thompson, "Herrnhut: A Prophetic Warning," SermonIndex, accessed April 21, 2022, https://www.sermonindex.net/modules/newbb/viewtopic.php?post_id=343370&topic_id=47848&forum=40.

[38] NKJV.

Made in the USA
Las Vegas, NV
03 February 2023

66798834R00066